Dear Mind
Whatever you
do to me.
I'll remain
proud of you

DATE: TIME:

OBSESSIVE COMPULSIVE PERSONALITY DISORDER
DAILY LOG

SITUATION / INTRUSIVE THOUGHTS :

_____
_____

MEANING OF THE INTRUSIVE THOUGHTS :

_____
_____

WHAT OCPD BEHAVIORS DID YOU DO ! !

_____
_____
_____
_____

Rate the Intensity of Obsessive Thoughts Today ○ ○ ○ ○ ○

MIND ENERGY : ☐ 🔋 ☐ 🔋 ☐ 🔋

OCPD DBT WORKSHEET

TODAY'S FICKLE FEELINGS AND MY COPING SKILLS USED

Date: / /
Sleep quality:

Daily Mood Checker ✓

- [ ] ANGRY
- [ ] ANNOYED
- [ ] ANXIOUS
- [ ] ASHAMED
- [ ] AWKWARD
- [ ] BRAVE
- [ ] CALM
- [ ] CHEERFUL
- [ ] CHILL
- [ ] CONFUSED
- [ ] DISCOURAGED
- [ ] DISTRACTED
- [ ] EMBARRASSED
- [ ] EXCITED
- [ ] FRIENDLY
- [ ] GUILTY
- [ ] HAPPY
- [ ] HOPEFUL
- [ ] LONELY
- [ ] LOVED
- [ ] NERVOUS
- [ ] OFFENDED
- [ ] SCARED
- [ ] THOUGHTFUL
- [ ] TIRED
- [ ] UNCOMFORTABLE
- [ ] UNSURE

CREATIVE OUTLETS TO REDUCE FEELINGS OF OBSESSION

THINGS TO WORK ON
(REALISTIC AND ACHIEVABLE THINGS)

THINGS I'M GRATEFUL FOR

IDEAS TO CONFRONT COMPULSIVE URGES

CHALLENGING OCPD SYMPTOMS DAILY ADVANCED WORKSHEET

CHALLENGE

The self-destructive obsessive habits that I (felt , do) today ,Determine your level of success in dealing with it :

_____
_____
_____
_____

Social activities I have been involved in.
How much did this contribute to my psychological comfort:

_____
_____
_____

Write down the good things you discovered about your personality today after practicing your social life,Things related to your self-esteem, dignity, and ways to develop them in the future:

_____
_____
_____

Are You Satisfied with Yourself Today: Yes ☐ No ☐

Why : _____

_____

NEGATIVE BEHAVIORS THAT I SHOULD GET RID

MY PRIORITIES, MY BOUNDARIES RELATED TO MY RELATIONSHIPS WITH OTHERS

DAILY WINS AGAINST OCPD

WAYS TO MAKE TOMORROW BETTER

OCPD BEHAVIORS TO FIX OR IMPROVE

ATTENTION AND SHYNESS MANAGEMENT

DISTRESS TOLERANCE SKILLS:

COMMUNICATION SKILLS WITH OTHERS:

INTERPERSONAL CONFLICTS

OTHER THINGS

UPDATED ACADEMIC FACTS, INFORMATIONS, ABOUT THE OBSESSIVE COMPULSIVE PERSONALITY DISORDER

TV SHOWS, ACADEMIC ARTICLES, SCIENTIFIC BOOKS,...ETC

DATE: TIME :

OBSESSIVE COMPULSIVE PERSONALITY DISORDER
DAILY LOG

SITUATION / INTRUSIVE THOUGHTS :

MEANING OF THE INTRUSIVE THOUGHTS :

WHAT OCPD BEHAVIORS DID YOU DO ! !

Rate the Intensity of Obsessive Thoughts Today ○ ○ ○ ○ ○

MIND ENERGY :

OCPD DBT WORKSHEET

TODAY'S FICKLE FEELINGS AND MY COPING SKILLS USED

Date: / /

Sleep quality:

Daily Mood Checker ✓

- ANGRY ☐
- ANNOYED ☐
- ANXIOUS ☐
- ASHAMED ☐
- AWKWARD ☐
- BRAVE ☐
- CALM ☐
- CHEERFUL ☐
- CHILL ☐
- CONFUSED ☐
- DISCOURAGED ☐
- DISTRACTED ☐
- EMBARRASSED ☐
- EXCITED ☐
- FRIENDLY ☐
- GUILTY ☐
- HAPPY ☐
- HOPEFUL ☐
- LONELY ☐
- LOVED ☐
- NERVOUS ☐
- OFFENDED ☐
- SCARED ☐
- THOUGHTFUL ☐
- TIRED ☐
- UNCOMFORTABLE ☐
- UNSURE ☐

CREATIVE OUTLETS TO REDUCE FEELINGS OF OBSESSION

**THINGS TO WORK ON
(REALISTIC AND ACHIEVABLE THINGS)**

THINGS I'M GRATEFUL FOR

IDEAS TO CONFRONT COMPULSIVE URGES

CHALLENGING OCPD SYMPTOMS DAILY ADVANCED WORKSHEET

CHALLENGE

_____

The self-destructive obsessive habits that I (felt , do) today ,Determine your level of success in dealing with it :

_____
_____
_____
_____

Social activities I have been involved in.
How much did this contribute to my psychological comfort:

_____
_____
_____

Write down the good things you discovered about your personality today after practicing your social life,Things related to your self-esteem, dignity, and ways to develop them in the future:

_____
_____
_____

Are You Satisfied with Yourself Today: Yes ☐ No ☐

Why : _____

_____

NEGATIVE BEHAVIORS THAT I SHOULD GET RID

MY PRIORITIES, MY BOUNDARIES RELATED TO MY RELATIONSHIPS WITH OTHERS

DAILY WINS AGAINST OCPD

WAYS TO MAKE TOMORROW BETTER

OCPD BEHAVIORS TO FIX OR IMPROVE

ATTENTION AND SHYNESS MANAGEMENT

DISTRESS TOLERANCE SKILLS:

COMMUNICATION SKILLS WITH OTHERS:

INTERPERSONAL CONFLICTS

OTHER THINGS

UPDATED ACADEMIC FACTS, INFORMATIONS, ABOUT THE OBSESSIVE COMPULSIVE PERSONALITY DISORDER

TV SHOWS, ACADEMIC ARTICLES, SCIENTIFIC BOOKS,...ETC

DATE: TIME:

OBSESSIVE COMPULSIVE PERSONALITY DISORDER
DAILY LOG

SITUATION / INTRUSIVE THOUGHTS :

_____

_____

MEANING OF THE INTRUSIVE THOUGHTS :

_____

_____

WHAT OCPD BEHAVIORS DID YOU DO ! !

_____

_____

_____

_____

Rate the Intensity of Obsessive Thoughts Today ○ ○ ○ ○ ○

MIND ENERGY :   ☐ 🔋   ☐ 🔋   ☐ 🔋

OCPD DBT WORKSHEET

TODAY'S FICKLE FEELINGS AND MY COPING SKILLS USED

Date: / /
Sleep quality:

Daily Mood Checker

- [ ] ANGRY
- [ ] ANNOYED
- [ ] ANXIOUS
- [ ] ASHAMED
- [ ] AWKWARD
- [ ] BRAVE
- [ ] CALM
- [ ] CHEERFUL
- [ ] CHILL
- [ ] CONFUSED
- [ ] DISCOURAGED
- [ ] DISTRACTED
- [ ] EMBARRASSED
- [ ] EXCITED
- [ ] FRIENDLY
- [ ] GUILTY
- [ ] HAPPY
- [ ] HOPEFUL
- [ ] LONELY
- [ ] LOVED
- [ ] NERVOUS
- [ ] OFFENDED
- [ ] SCARED
- [ ] THOUGHTFUL
- [ ] TIRED
- [ ] UNCOMFORTABLE
- [ ] UNSURE

CREATIVE OUTLETS TO REDUCE FEELINGS OF OBSESSION

THINGS TO WORK ON
(REALISTIC AND ACHIEVABLE THINGS)

THINGS I'M GRATFUL FOR

IDEAS TO CONFRONT COMPULSIVE URGES

CHALLENGING OCPD SYMPTOMS DAILY ADVANCED WORKSHEET

CHALLENGE

The self-destructive obsessive habits that I (felt , do) today ,Determine your level of success in dealing with it :

_____
_____
_____
_____

Social activities I have been involved in.
How much did this contribute to my psychological comfort:

_____
_____
_____

Write down the good things you discovered about your personality today after practicing your social life,Things related to your self-esteem, dignity, and ways to develop them in the future:

_____
_____
_____

Yes No
☐ ☐

Are You Satisfied with Yourself Today:

Why : _____

_____

DATE: TIME :

OBSESSIVE COMPULSIVE PERSONALITY DISORDER
DAILY LOG

SITUATION / INTRUSIVE THOUGHTS :

MEANING OF THE INTRUSIVE THOUGHTS :

WHAT OCPD BEHAVIORS DID YOU DO ! !

Rate the Intensity of Obsessive Thoughts Today ○ ○ ○ ○ ○

MIND ENERGY :

OCPD DBT WORKSHEET

TODAY'S FICKLE FEELINGS AND MY COPING SKILLS USED

Date: / /
Sleep quality:

Daily Mood Checker ✓

- ANGRY ☐
- ANNOYED ☐
- ANXIOUS ☐
- ASHAMED ☐
- AWKWARD ☐
- BRAVE ☐
- CALM ☐
- CHEERFUL ☐
- CHILL ☐
- CONFUSED ☐
- DISCOURAGED ☐
- DISTRACTED ☐
- EMBARRASSED ☐
- EXCITED ☐
- FRIENDLY ☐
- GUILTY ☐
- HAPPY ☐
- HOPEFUL ☐
- LONELY ☐
- LOVED ☐
- NERVOUS ☐
- OFFENDED ☐
- SCARED ☐
- THOUGHTFUL ☐
- TIRED ☐
- UNCOMFORTABLE ☐
- UNSURE ☐

CREATIVE OUTLETS TO REDUCE FEELINGS OF OBSESSION

THINGS TO WORK ON
(REALISTIC AND ACHIEVABLE THINGS)

THINGS I'M GRATFUL FOR

IDEAS TO CONFRONT COMPULSIVE URGES

CHALLENGING OCPD SYMPTOMS DAILY ADVANCED WORKSHEET

CHALLENGE

_____

The self-destructive obsessive habits that I (felt , do) today ,Determine your level of success in dealing with it :

_____
_____
_____
_____

Social activities I have been involved in.
How much did this contribute to my psychological comfort:

_____
_____
_____

Write down the good things you discovered about your personality today after practicing your social life,Things related to your self-esteem, dignity, and ways to develop them in the future:

_____
_____
_____

Are You Satisfied with Yourself Today: Yes ☐ No ☐

Why : _____

_____

NEGATIVE BEHAVIORS THAT I SHOULD GET RID

MY PRIORITIES, MY BOUNDARIES RELATED TO MY RELATIONSHIPS WITH OTHERS

DAILY WINS AGAINST OCPD

_____

_____

_____

_____

_____

_____

_____

WAYS TO MAKE TOMORROW BETTER

_____

_____

_____

_____

_____

_____

OCPD BEHAVIORS TO FIX OR IMPROVE

ATTENTION AND SHYNESS MANAGEMENT

DISTRESS TOLERANCE SKILLS:

COMMUNICATION SKILLS WITH OTHERS:

INTERPERSONAL CONFLICTS

OTHER THINGS

UPDATED ACADEMIC FACTS, INFORMATIONS, ABOUT THE OBSESSIVE COMPULSIVE PERSONALITY DISORDER

TV SHOWS, ACADEMIC ARTICLES, SCIENTIFIC BOOKS,...ETC

DATE: TIME :

OBSESSIVE COMPULSIVE PERSONALITY DISORDER
DAILY LOG

SITUATION / INTRUSIVE THOUGHTS :

MEANING OF THE INTRUSIVE THOUGHTS :

WHAT OCPD BEHAVIORS DID YOU DO ! !

Rate the Intensity of Obsessive Thoughts Today ○ ○ ○ ○ ○

MIND ENERGY :

OCPD DBT WORKSHEET

TODAY'S FICKLE FEELINGS AND MY COPING SKILLS USED

Date: / /

Sleep quality:

Daily Mood Checker ✓

- ANGRY ☐
- ANNOYED ☐
- ANXIOUS ☐
- ASHAMED ☐
- AWKWARD ☐
- BRAVE ☐
- CALM ☐
- CHEERFUL ☐
- CHILL ☐
- CONFUSED ☐
- DISCOURAGED ☐
- DISTRACTED ☐
- EMBARRASSED ☐
- EXCITED ☐
- FRIENDLY ☐
- GUILTY ☐
- HAPPY ☐
- HOPEFUL ☐
- LONELY ☐
- LOVED ☐
- NERVOUS ☐
- OFFENDED ☐
- SCARED ☐
- THOUGHTFUL ☐
- TIRED ☐
- UNCOMFORTABLE ☐
- UNSURE ☐

CREATIVE OUTLETS TO REDUCE FEELINGS OF OBSESSION

THINGS TO WORK ON
(REALISTIC AND ACHIEVABLE THINGS)

THINGS I'M GRATEFUL FOR

IDEAS TO CONFRONT COMPULSIVE URGES

CHALLENGING OCPD SYMPTOMS DAILY ADVANCED WORKSHEET

CHALLENGE

The self-destructive obsessive habits that I (felt , do) today ,Determine your level of success in dealing with it :

_____
_____
_____
_____

Social activities I have been involved in.
How much did this contribute to my psychological comfort:

_____
_____
_____

Write down the good things you discovered about your personality today after practicing your social life,Things related to your self-esteem, dignity, and ways to develop them in the future:

_____
_____
_____

Yes No
☐ ☐

Are You Satisfied with Yourself Today:

Why : _____

_____

DATE: TIME :

OBSESSIVE COMPULSIVE PERSONALITY DISORDER
DAILY LOG

SITUATION / INTRUSIVE THOUGHTS :

_____

_____

MEANING OF THE INTRUSIVE THOUGHTS :

_____

_____

WHAT OCPD BEHAVIORS DID YOU DO ! !

_____

_____

_____

_____

Rate the Intensity of Obsessive Thoughts Today ○ ○ ○ ○ ○

MIND ENERGY :   ☐ 🔋   ☐ 🔋   ☐ 🔋

OCPD DBT WORKSHEET

TODAY'S FICKLE FEELINGS AND MY COPING SKILLS USED

Date: / /
Sleep quality:

Daily Mood Checker ✓

- ANGRY ☐
- ANNOYED ☐
- ANXIOUS ☐
- ASHAMED ☐
- AWKWARD ☐
- BRAVE ☐
- CALM ☐
- CHEERFUL ☐
- CHILL ☐
- CONFUSED ☐
- DISCOURAGED ☐
- DISTRACTED ☐
- EMBARRASSED ☐
- EXCITED ☐
- FRIENDLY ☐
- GUILTY ☐
- HAPPY ☐
- HOPEFUL ☐
- LONELY ☐
- LOVED ☐
- NERVOUS ☐
- OFFENDED ☐
- SCARED ☐
- THOUGHTFUL ☐
- TIRED ☐
- UNCOMFORTABLE ☐
- UNSURE ☐

CREATIVE OUTLETS TO REDUCE FEELINGS OF OBSESSION

THINGS TO WORK ON
(REALISTIC AND ACHIEVABLE THINGS)

THINGS I'M GRATEFUL FOR

IDEAS TO CONFRONT COMPULSIVE URGES

CHALLENGING OCPD SYMPTOMS DAILY ADVANCED WORKSHEET

CHALLENGE

The self-destructive obsessive habits that I (felt , do) today ,Determine your level of success in dealing with it :

_____
_____
_____
_____

Social activities I have been involved in.
How much did this contribute to my psychological comfort:

_____
_____
_____

Write down the good things you discovered about your personality today after practicing your social life,Things related to your self-esteem, dignity, and ways to develop them in the future:

_____
_____
_____

Are You Satisfied with Yourself Today: Yes ☐ No ☐

Why : _____

_____

NEGATIVE BEHAVIORS THAT I SHOULD GET RID

MY PRIORITIES, MY BOUNDARIES RELATED TO MY RELATIONSHIPS WITH OTHERS

DAILY WINS AGAINST OCPD

WAYS TO MAKE TOMORROW BETTER

OCPD BEHAVIORS TO FIX OR IMPROVE

ATTENTION AND SHYNESS MANAGEMENT

DISTRESS TOLERANCE SKILLS:

COMMUNICATION SKILLS WITH OTHERS:

INTERPERSONAL CONFLICTS

OTHER THINGS

UPDATED ACADEMIC FACTS, INFORMATIONS, ABOUT THE OBSESSIVE COMPULSIVE PERSONALITY DISORDER

TV SHOWS, ACADEMIC ARTICLES, SCIENTIFIC BOOKS,...ETC

DATE: TIME :

OBSESSIVE COMPULSIVE PERSONALITY DISORDER
DAILY LOG

SITUATION / INTRUSIVE THOUGHTS :

_____

_____

_____

MEANING OF THE INTRUSIVE THOUGHTS :

_____

_____

_____

WHAT OCPD BEHAVIORS DID YOU DO ! !

_____

_____

_____

_____

Rate the Intensity of Obsessive Thoughts Today ◯ ◯ ◯ ◯ ◯

MIND ENERGY :   ☐ 🔋   ☐ 🔋   ☐ 🔋

OCPD DBT WORKSHEET

TODAY'S FICKLE FEELINGS AND MY COPING SKILLS USED

Date: / /

Sleep quality:

Daily Mood Checker

- ANGRY ☐
- ANNOYED ☐
- ANXIOUS ☐
- ASHAMED ☐
- AWKWARD ☐
- BRAVE ☐
- CALM ☐
- CHEERFUL ☐
- CHILL ☐
- CONFUSED ☐
- DISCOURAGED ☐
- DISTRACTED ☐
- EMBARRASSED ☐
- EXCITED ☐
- FRIENDLY ☐
- GUILTY ☐
- HAPPY ☐
- HOPEFUL ☐
- LONELY ☐
- LOVED ☐
- NERVOUS ☐
- OFFENDED ☐
- SCARED ☐
- THOUGHTFUL ☐
- TIRED ☐
- UNCOMFORTABLE ☐
- UNSURE ☐

CREATIVE OUTLETS TO REDUCE FEELINGS OF OBSESSION

THINGS TO WORK ON
(REALISTIC AND ACHIEVABLE THINGS)

THINGS I'M GRATEFUL FOR

IDEAS TO CONFRONT COMPULSIVE URGES

CHALLENGING OCPD SYMPTOMS DAILY ADVANCED WORKSHEET

CHALLENGE

The self-destructive obsessive habits that I (felt , do) today ,Determine your level of success in dealing with it :

_____
_____
_____
_____

Social activities I have been involved in.
How much did this contribute to my psychological comfort:

_____
_____
_____

Write down the good things you discovered about your personality today after practicing your social life, Things related to your self-esteem, dignity, and ways to develop them in the future:

_____
_____
_____

Are You Satisfied with Yourself Today: Yes ☐ No ☐

Why : _____

_____

DATE: TIME:

OBSESSIVE COMPULSIVE PERSONALITY DISORDER
DAILY LOG

SITUATION / INTRUSIVE THOUGHTS :

MEANING OF THE INTRUSIVE THOUGHTS :

WHAT OCPD BEHAVIORS DID YOU DO ! !

Rate the Intensity of Obsessive Thoughts Today ○ ○ ○ ○ ○

MIND ENERGY :

OCPD DBT WORKSHEET

TODAY'S FICKLE FEELINGS AND MY COPING SKILLS USED

Date: / /
Sleep quality:

Daily Mood Checker ✓

- ANGRY ☐
- ANNOYED ☐
- ANXIOUS ☐
- ASHAMED ☐
- AWKWARD ☐
- BRAVE ☐
- CALM ☐
- CHEERFUL ☐
- CHILL ☐
- CONFUSED ☐
- DISCOURAGED ☐
- DISTRACTED ☐
- EMBARRASSED ☐
- EXCITED ☐
- FRIENDLY ☐
- GUILTY ☐
- HAPPY ☐
- HOPEFUL ☐
- LONELY ☐
- LOVED ☐
- NERVOUS ☐
- OFFENDED ☐
- SCARED ☐
- THOUGHTFUL ☐
- TIRED ☐
- UNCOMFORTABLE ☐
- UNSURE ☐

CREATIVE OUTLETS TO REDUCE FEELINGS OF OBSESSION

THINGS TO WORK ON
(REALISTIC AND ACHIEVABLE THINGS)

THINGS I'M GRATEFUL FOR

IDEAS TO CONFRONT COMPULSIVE URGES

CHALLENGING OCPD SYMPTOMS DAILY ADVANCED WORKSHEET

CHALLENGE

The self-destructive obsessive habits that I (felt , do) today ,Determine your level of success in dealing with it :

_____
_____
_____
_____

Social activities I have been involved in.
How much did this contribute to my psychological comfort:

_____
_____
_____

Write down the good things you discovered about your personality today after practicing your social life,Things related to your self-esteem, dignity, and ways to develop them in the future:

_____
_____
_____

Are You Satisfied with Yourself Today: Yes ☐ No ☐

Why : _____

_____

NEGATIVE BEHAVIORS THAT I SHOULD GET RID

MY PRIORITIES, MY BOUNDARIES RELATED TO MY RELATIONSHIPS WITH OTHERS

DAILY WINS AGAINST OCPD

WAYS TO MAKE TOMORROW BETTER

OCPD BEHAVIORS TO FIX OR IMPROVE

ATTENTION AND SHYNESS MANAGEMENT

DISTRESS TOLERANCE SKILLS:

COMMUNICATION SKILLS WITH OTHERS:

INTERPERSONAL CONFLICTS

OTHER THINGS

UPDATED ACADEMIC FACTS, INFORMATIONS, ABOUT THE OBSESSIVE COMPULSIVE PERSONALITY DISORDER

TV SHOWS, ACADEMIC ARTICLES, SCIENTIFIC BOOKS,...ETC

DATE: TIME:

OBSESSIVE COMPULSIVE PERSONALITY DISORDER
DAILY LOG

SITUATION / INTRUSIVE THOUGHTS :

MEANING OF THE INTRUSIVE THOUGHTS :

WHAT OCPD BEHAVIORS DID YOU DO ! !

Rate the Intensity of Obsessive Thoughts Today ○ ○ ○ ○ ○

MIND ENERGY : ☐ 🔋 ☐ 🔋 ☐ 🔋

OCPD DBT WORKSHEET

TODAY'S FICKLE FEELINGS AND MY COPING SKILLS USED

Date: / /

Sleep quality:

Daily Mood Checker

- ANGRY ☐
- ANNOYED ☐
- ANXIOUS ☐
- ASHAMED ☐
- AWKWARD ☐
- BRAVE ☐
- CALM ☐
- CHEERFUL ☐
- CHILL ☐
- CONFUSED ☐
- DISCOURAGED ☐
- DISTRACTED ☐
- EMBARRASSED ☐
- EXCITED ☐
- FRIENDLY ☐
- GUILTY ☐
- HAPPY ☐
- HOPEFUL ☐
- LONELY ☐
- LOVED ☐
- NERVOUS ☐
- OFFENDED ☐
- SCARED ☐
- THOUGHTFUL ☐
- TIRED ☐
- UNCOMFORTABLE ☐
- UNSURE ☐

CREATIVE OUTLETS TO REDUCE FEELINGS OF OBSESSION

THINGS TO WORK ON
(REALISTIC AND ACHIEVABLE THINGS)

THINGS I'M GRATFUL FOR

IDEAS TO CONFRONT COMPULSIVE URGES

CHALLENGING OCPD SYMPTOMS DAILY ADVANCED WORKSHEET

CHALLENGE

_____

The self-destructive obsessive habits that I (felt , do) today ,Determine your level of success in dealing with it :

_____
_____
_____
_____

Social activities I have been involved in.
How much did this contribute to my psychological comfort:

_____
_____
_____

Write down the good things you discovered about your personality today after practicing your social life, Things related to your self-esteem, dignity, and ways to develop them in the future:

_____
_____
_____

Are You Satisfied with Yourself Today: Yes ☐ No ☐

Why : _____
_____

DATE: TIME :

OBSESSIVE COMPULSIVE PERSONALITY DISORDER
DAILY LOG

SITUATION / INTRUSIVE THOUGHTS :

MEANING OF THE INTRUSIVE THOUGHTS :

WHAT OCPD BEHAVIORS DID YOU DO ! !

_____

_____

_____

_____

Rate the Intensity of Obsessive Thoughts Today   ○ ○ ○ ○ ○

| MIND ENERGY : | ☐ 🔋 | ☐ 🔋 | ☐ 🔋 |

OCPD DBT WORKSHEET

TODAY'S FICKLE FEELINGS AND MY COPING SKILLS USED

Date: / /
Sleep quality:

Daily Mood Checker

- ANGRY ☐
- ANNOYED ☐
- ANXIOUS ☐
- ASHAMED ☐
- AWKWARD ☐
- BRAVE ☐
- CALM ☐
- CHEERFUL ☐
- CHILL ☐
- CONFUSED ☐
- DISCOURAGED ☐
- DISTRACTED ☐
- EMBARRASSED ☐
- EXCITED ☐
- FRIENDLY ☐
- GUILTY ☐
- HAPPY ☐
- HOPEFUL ☐
- LONELY ☐
- LOVED ☐
- NERVOUS ☐
- OFFENDED ☐
- SCARED ☐
- THOUGHTFUL ☐
- TIRED ☐
- UNCOMFORTABLE ☐
- UNSURE ☐

CREATIVE OUTLETS TO REDUCE FEELINGS OF OBSESSION

THINGS TO WORK ON
(REALISTIC AND ACHIEVABLE THINGS)

THINGS I'M GRATEFUL FOR

IDEAS TO CONFRONT COMPULSIVE URGES

CHALLENGING OCPD SYMPTOMS DAILY ADVANCED WORKSHEET

CHALLENGE

The self-destructive obsessive habits that I (felt , do) today ,Determine your level of success in dealing with it :

_____
_____
_____
_____

Social activities I have been involved in.
How much did this contribute to my psychological comfort:

_____
_____
_____

Write down the good things you discovered about your personality today after practicing your social life,Things related to your self-esteem, dignity, and ways to develop them in the future:

_____
_____
_____

Are You Satisfied with Yourself Today: Yes ☐ No ☐

Why : _____

_____

NEGATIVE BEHAVIORS THAT I SHOULD GET RID

MY PRIORITIES, MY BOUNDARIES RELATED TO MY RELATIONSHIPS WITH OTHERS

DAILY WINS AGAINST OCPD

_____
_____
_____
_____
_____
_____
_____

WAYS TO MAKE TOMORROW BETTER

_____
_____
_____
_____
_____

OCPD BEHAVIORS TO FIX OR IMPROVE

ATTENTION AND SHYNESS MANAGEMENT

DISTRESS TOLERANCE SKILLS:

COMMUNICATION SKILLS WITH OTHERS:

INTERPERSONAL CONFLICTS

OTHER THINGS

UPDATED ACADEMIC FACTS, INFORMATIONS, ABOUT THE OBSESSIVE COMPULSIVE PERSONALITY DISORDER

TV SHOWS, ACADEMIC ARTICLES, SCIENTIFIC BOOKS,...ETC

DATE: TIME :

OBSESSIVE COMPULSIVE PERSONALITY DISORDER
DAILY LOG

SITUATION / INTRUSIVE THOUGHTS :

_____

_____

_____

MEANING OF THE INTRUSIVE THOUGHTS :

_____

_____

_____

WHAT OCPD BEHAVIORS DID YOU DO ! !

_____

_____

_____

_____

Rate the Intensity of Obsessive Thoughts Today   ○ ○ ○ ○ ○

MIND ENERGY :   ☐ 🔋   ☐ 🔋   ☐ 🔋

OCPD DBT WORKSHEET

TODAY'S FICKLE FEELINGS AND MY COPING SKILLS USED

Date: / /

Sleep quality:

Daily Mood Checker ✓

- ANGRY ☐
- ANNOYED ☐
- ANXIOUS ☐
- ASHAMED ☐
- AWKWARD ☐
- BRAVE ☐
- CALM ☐
- CHEERFUL ☐
- CHILL ☐
- CONFUSED ☐
- DISCOURAGED ☐
- DISTRACTED ☐
- EMBARRASSED ☐
- EXCITED ☐
- FRIENDLY ☐
- GUILTY ☐
- HAPPY ☐
- HOPEFUL ☐
- LONELY ☐
- LOVED ☐
- NERVOUS ☐
- OFFENDED ☐
- SCARED ☐
- THOUGHTFUL ☐
- TIRED ☐
- UNCOMFORTABLE ☐
- UNSURE ☐

CREATIVE OUTLETS TO REDUCE FEELINGS OF OBSESSION

THINGS TO WORK ON
(REALISTIC AND ACHIEVABLE THINGS)

THINGS I'M GRATFUL FOR

IDEAS TO CONFRONT COMPULSIVE URGES

CHALLENGING OCPD SYMPTOMS DAILY ADVANCED WORKSHEET

CHALLENGE

The self-destructive obsessive habits that I (felt , do) today ,Determine your level of success in dealing with it :

_____
_____
_____
_____

Social activities I have been involved in.
How much did this contribute to my psychological comfort:

_____
_____
_____

Write down the good things you discovered about your personality today after practicing your social life,Things related to your self-esteem, dignity, and ways to develop them in the future:

_____
_____
_____

Are You Satisfied with Yourself Today: Yes ☐ No ☐

Why : _____
_____

DATE: TIME:

OBSESSIVE COMPULSIVE PERSONALITY DISORDER
DAILY LOG

SITUATION / INTRUSIVE THOUGHTS :

MEANING OF THE INTRUSIVE THOUGHTS :

WHAT OCPD BEHAVIORS DID YOU DO ! !

Rate the Intensity of Obsessive Thoughts Today ○ ○ ○ ○ ○

MIND ENERGY :

OCPD DBT WORKSHEET

TODAY'S FICKLE FEELINGS AND MY COPING SKILLS USED

Date: / /

Sleep quality:

Daily Mood Checker ✓

- ANGRY ☐
- ANNOYED ☐
- ANXIOUS ☐
- ASHAMED ☐
- AWKWARD ☐
- BRAVE ☐
- CALM ☐
- CHEERFUL ☐
- CHILL ☐
- CONFUSED ☐
- DISCOURAGED ☐
- DISTRACTED ☐
- EMBARRASSED ☐
- EXCITED ☐
- FRIENDLY ☐
- GUILTY ☐
- HAPPY ☐
- HOPEFUL ☐
- LONELY ☐
- LOVED ☐
- NERVOUS ☐
- OFFENDED ☐
- SCARED ☐
- THOUGHTFUL ☐
- TIRED ☐
- UNCOMFORTABLE ☐
- UNSURE ☐

CREATIVE OUTLETS TO REDUCE FEELINGS OF OBSESSION

THINGS TO WORK ON
(REALISTIC AND ACHIEVABLE THINGS)

THINGS I'M GRATEFUL FOR

IDEAS TO CONFRONT COMPULSIVE URGES

CHALLENGING OCPD SYMPTOMS DAILY ADVANCED WORKSHEET

CHALLENGE
OPEN

The self-destructive obsessive habits that I (felt , do) today ,Determine your level of success in dealing with it :

_____

_____

_____

_____

Social activities I have been involved in.
How much did this contribute to my psychological comfort:

_____

_____

_____

Write down the good things you discovered about your personality today after practicing your social life,Things related to your self-esteem, dignity, and ways to develop them in the future:

_____

_____

_____

Are You Satisfied with Yourself Today: Yes ☐   No ☐

Why : _____

_____

NEGATIVE BEHAVIORS THAT I SHOULD GET RID

MY PRIORITIES, MY BOUNDARIES RELATED TO MY RELATIONSHIPS WITH OTHERS

DAILY WINS AGAINST OCPD

WAYS TO MAKE TOMORROW BETTER

OCPD BEHAVIORS TO FIX OR IMPROVE

ATTENTION AND SHYNESS MANAGEMENT

DISTRESS TOLERANCE SKILLS:

COMMUNICATION SKILLS WITH OTHERS:

INTERPERSONAL CONFLICTS

OTHER THINGS

UPDATED ACADEMIC FACTS, INFORMATIONS, ABOUT THE OBSESSIVE COMPULSIVE PERSONALITY DISORDER

TV SHOWS, ACADEMIC ARTICLES, SCIENTIFIC BOOKS,...ETC

DATE: TIME :

OBSESSIVE COMPULSIVE PERSONALITY DISORDER
DAILY LOG

SITUATION / INTRUSIVE THOUGHTS :

MEANING OF THE INTRUSIVE THOUGHTS :

WHAT OCPD BEHAVIORS DID YOU DO ! !

Rate the Intensity of Obsessive Thoughts Today ○ ○ ○ ○ ○ ○

MIND ENERGY : ☐ 🔋 ☐ 🔋 ☐ 🔋

OCPD DBT WORKSHEET

TODAY'S FICKLE FEELINGS AND MY COPING SKILLS USED

Date: / /
Sleep quality:

Daily Mood Checker

- ANGRY ☐
- ANNOYED ☐
- ANXIOUS ☐
- ASHAMED ☐
- AWKWARD ☐
- BRAVE ☐
- CALM ☐
- CHEERFUL ☐
- CHILL ☐
- CONFUSED ☐
- DISCOURAGED ☐
- DISTRACTED ☐
- EMBARRASSED ☐
- EXCITED ☐
- FRIENDLY ☐
- GUILTY ☐
- HAPPY ☐
- HOPEFUL ☐
- LONELY ☐
- LOVED ☐
- NERVOUS ☐
- OFFENDED ☐
- SCARED ☐
- THOUGHTFUL ☐
- TIRED ☐
- UNCOMFORTABLE ☐
- UNSURE ☐

CREATIVE OUTLETS TO REDUCE FEELINGS OF OBSESSION

THINGS TO WORK ON
(REALISTIC AND ACHIEVABLE THINGS)

THINGS I'M GRATEFUL FOR

IDEAS TO CONFRONT COMPULSIVE URGES

CHALLENGING OCPD SYMPTOMS DAILY ADVANCED WORKSHEET

CHALLENGE

The self-destructive obsessive habits that I (felt , do) today ,Determine your level of success in dealing with it :

_____

_____

_____

_____

Social activities I have been involved in.
How much did this contribute to my psychological comfort:

_____

_____

_____

Write down the good things you discovered about your personality today after practicing your social life,Things related to your self-esteem, dignity, and ways to develop them in the future:

_____

_____

_____

Are You Satisfied with Yourself Today: Yes ☐ No ☐

Why : _____

_____

DATE: TIME :

OBSESSIVE COMPULSIVE PERSONALITY DISORDER
DAILY LOG

SITUATION / INTRUSIVE THOUGHTS :

_____

_____

_____

MEANING OF THE INTRUSIVE THOUGHTS :

_____

_____

_____

WHAT OCPD BEHAVIORS DID YOU DO ! !

_____

_____

_____

_____

Rate the Intensity of Obsessive Thoughts Today ○ ○ ○ ○ ○

MIND ENERGY :   ☐ 🔋   ☐ 🔋   ☐ 🔋

OCPD DBT WORKSHEET

TODAY'S FICKLE FEELINGS AND MY COPING SKILLS USED

CREATIVE OUTLETS TO REDUCE FEELINGS OF OBSESSION

THINGS TO WORK ON
(REALISTIC AND ACHIEVABLE THINGS)

THINGS I'M GRATFUL FOR

IDEAS TO CONFRONT COMPULSIVE URGES

Date: / /

Sleep quality:

Daily Mood Checker

- [ ] ANGRY
- [ ] ANNOYED
- [ ] ANXIOUS
- [ ] ASHAMED
- [ ] AWKWARD
- [ ] BRAVE
- [ ] CALM
- [ ] CHEERFUL
- [ ] CHILL
- [ ] CONFUSED
- [ ] DISCOURAGED
- [ ] DISTRACTED
- [ ] EMBARRASSED
- [ ] EXCITED
- [ ] FRIENDLY
- [ ] GUILTY
- [ ] HAPPY
- [ ] HOPEFUL
- [ ] LONELY
- [ ] LOVED
- [ ] NERVOUS
- [ ] OFFENDED
- [ ] SCARED
- [ ] THOUGHTFUL
- [ ] TIRED
- [ ] UNCOMFORTABLE
- [ ] UNSURE

CHALLENGING OCPD SYMPTOMS DAILY ADVANCED WORKSHEET

CHALLENGE

The self-destructive obsessive habits that I (felt , do) today ,Determine your level of success in dealing with it :

_____
_____
_____
_____

Social activities I have been involved in.
How much did this contribute to my psychological comfort:

_____
_____
_____

Write down the good things you discovered about your personality today after practicing your social life,Things related to your self-esteem, dignity, and ways to develop them in the future:

_____
_____
_____

Are You Satisfied with Yourself Today: Yes ☐ No ☐

Why : _____

_____

NEGATIVE BEHAVIORS THAT I SHOULD GET RID

MY PRIORITIES, MY BOUNDARIES RELATED TO MY RELATIONSHIPS WITH OTHERS

DAILY WINS AGAINST OCPD

WAYS TO MAKE TOMORROW BETTER

OCPD BEHAVIORS TO FIX OR IMPROVE

ATTENTION AND SHYNESS MANAGEMENT

DISTRESS TOLERANCE SKILLS:

COMMUNICATION SKILLS WITH OTHERS:

INTERPERSONAL CONFLICTS

OTHER THINGS

UPDATED ACADEMIC FACTS, INFORMATIONS, ABOUT THE OBSESSIVE COMPULSIVE PERSONALITY DISORDER

TV SHOWS, ACADEMIC ARTICLES, SCIENTIFIC BOOKS,...ETC

DATE: TIME :

OBSESSIVE COMPULSIVE PERSONALITY DISORDER
DAILY LOG

SITUATION / INTRUSIVE THOUGHTS :

MEANING OF THE INTRUSIVE THOUGHTS :

WHAT OCPD BEHAVIORS DID YOU DO ! !

Rate the Intensity of Obsessive Thoughts Today ○ ○ ○ ○ ○

MIND ENERGY :

OCPD DBT WORKSHEET

TODAY'S FICKLE FEELINGS AND MY COPING SKILLS USED

CREATIVE OUTLETS TO REDUCE FEELINGS OF OBSESSION

THINGS TO WORK ON
(REALISTIC AND ACHIEVABLE THINGS)

THINGS I'M GRATEFUL FOR

IDEAS TO CONFRONT COMPULSIVE URGES

Date: / /
Sleep quality:

Daily Mood Checker

- [ ] ANGRY
- [ ] ANNOYED
- [ ] ANXIOUS
- [ ] ASHAMED
- [ ] AWKWARD
- [ ] BRAVE
- [ ] CALM
- [ ] CHEERFUL
- [ ] CHILL
- [ ] CONFUSED
- [ ] DISCOURAGED
- [ ] DISTRACTED
- [ ] EMBARRASSED
- [ ] EXCITED
- [ ] FRIENDLY
- [ ] GUILTY
- [ ] HAPPY
- [ ] HOPEFUL
- [ ] LONELY
- [ ] LOVED
- [ ] NERVOUS
- [ ] OFFENDED
- [ ] SCARED
- [ ] THOUGHTFUL
- [ ] TIRED
- [ ] UNCOMFORTABLE
- [ ] UNSURE

CHALLENGING OCPD SYMPTOMS DAILY ADVANCED WORKSHEET

CHALLENGE

_____

The self-destructive obsessive habits that I (felt , do) today ,Determine your level of success in dealing with it :

_____
_____
_____
_____

Social activities I have been involved in.
How much did this contribute to my psychological comfort:

_____
_____
_____

Write down the good things you discovered about your personality today after practicing your social life,Things related to your self-esteem, dignity, and ways to develop them in the future:

_____
_____
_____

Are You Satisfied with Yourself Today: Yes ☐ No ☐

Why : _____

_____

DATE: TIME:

OBSESSIVE COMPULSIVE PERSONALITY DISORDER
DAILY LOG

SITUATION / INTRUSIVE THOUGHTS :

MEANING OF THE INTRUSIVE THOUGHTS :

WHAT OCPD BEHAVIORS DID YOU DO ! !

Rate the Intensity of Obsessive Thoughts Today   ○ ○ ○ ○ ○

MIND ENERGY :   ☐ 🔋   ☐ 🔋   ☐ 🔋

OCPD DBT WORKSHEET

Date: / /
Sleep quality:

TODAY'S FICKLE FEELINGS AND MY COPING SKILLS USED

CREATIVE OUTLETS TO REDUCE FEELINGS OF OBSESSION

THINGS TO WORK ON
(REALISTIC AND ACHIEVABLE THINGS)

THINGS I'M GRATEFUL FOR

IDEAS TO CONFRONT COMPULSIVE URGES

Daily Mood Checker ✓

- [ ] ANGRY
- [ ] ANNOYED
- [ ] ANXIOUS
- [ ] ASHAMED
- [ ] AWKWARD
- [ ] BRAVE
- [ ] CALM
- [ ] CHEERFUL
- [ ] CHILL
- [ ] CONFUSED
- [ ] DISCOURAGED
- [ ] DISTRACTED
- [ ] EMBARRASSED
- [ ] EXCITED
- [ ] FRIENDLY
- [ ] GUILTY
- [ ] HAPPY
- [ ] HOPEFUL
- [ ] LONELY
- [ ] LOVED
- [ ] NERVOUS
- [ ] OFFENDED
- [ ] SCARED
- [ ] THOUGHTFUL
- [ ] TIRED
- [ ] UNCOMFORTABLE
- [ ] UNSURE

CHALLENGING OCPD SYMPTOMS DAILY ADVANCED WORKSHEET

CHALLENGE

The self-destructive obsessive habits that I (felt , do) today ,Determine your level of success in dealing with it :

_____
_____
_____
_____

Social activities I have been involved in.
How much did this contribute to my psychological comfort:

_____
_____
_____

Write down the good things you discovered about your personality today after practicing your social life,Things related to your self-esteem, dignity, and ways to develop them in the future:

_____
_____
_____

Are You Satisfied with Yourself Today: Yes ☐ No ☐

Why : _____

_____

NEGATIVE BEHAVIORS THAT I SHOULD GET RID

MY PRIORITIES, MY BOUNDARIES RELATED TO MY RELATIONSHIPS WITH OTHERS

DAILY WINS AGAINST OCPD

_____

_____

_____

_____

_____

_____

_____

WAYS TO MAKE TOMORROW BETTER

_____

_____

_____

_____

_____

_____

OCPD BEHAVIORS TO FIX OR IMPROVE

ATTENTION AND SHYNESS MANAGEMENT

DISTRESS TOLERANCE SKILLS:

COMMUNICATION SKILLS WITH OTHERS:

INTERPERSONAL CONFLICTS

OTHER THINGS

UPDATED ACADEMIC FACTS, INFORMATIONS, ABOUT THE OBSESSIVE COMPULSIVE PERSONALITY DISORDER

TV SHOWS, ACADEMIC ARTICLES, SCIENTIFIC BOOKS,...ETC

DATE: TIME :

OBSESSIVE COMPULSIVE PERSONALITY DISORDER
DAILY LOG

SITUATION / INTRUSIVE THOUGHTS :

MEANING OF THE INTRUSIVE THOUGHTS :

WHAT OCPD BEHAVIORS DID YOU DO ! !

Rate the Intensity of Obsessive Thoughts Today ○ ○ ○ ○ ○

MIND ENERGY : ☐ 🔋   ☐ 🔋   ☐ 🔋

OCPD DBT WORKSHEET

TODAY'S FICKLE FEELINGS AND MY COPING SKILLS USED

Date: / /

Sleep quality:

Daily Mood Checker

- [ ] ANGRY
- [ ] ANNOYED
- [ ] ANXIOUS
- [ ] ASHAMED
- [ ] AWKWARD
- [ ] BRAVE
- [ ] CALM
- [ ] CHEERFUL
- [ ] CHILL
- [ ] CONFUSED
- [ ] DISCOURAGED
- [ ] DISTRACTED
- [ ] EMBARRASSED
- [ ] EXCITED
- [ ] FRIENDLY
- [ ] GUILTY
- [ ] HAPPY
- [ ] HOPEFUL
- [ ] LONELY
- [ ] LOVED
- [ ] NERVOUS
- [ ] OFFENDED
- [ ] SCARED
- [ ] THOUGHTFUL
- [ ] TIRED
- [ ] UNCOMFORTABLE
- [ ] UNSURE

CREATIVE OUTLETS TO REDUCE FEELINGS OF OBSESSION

THINGS TO WORK ON
(REALISTIC AND ACHIEVABLE THINGS)

THINGS I'M GRATEFUL FOR

IDEAS TO CONFRONT COMPULSIVE URGES

CHALLENGING OCPD SYMPTOMS DAILY ADVANCED WORKSHEET

CHALLENGE

The self-destructive obsessive habits that I (felt , do) today ,Determine your level of success in dealing with it :

_____
_____
_____
_____

Social activities I have been involved in.
How much did this contribute to my psychological comfort:

_____
_____
_____

Write down the good things you discovered about your personality today after practicing your social life,Things related to your self-esteem, dignity, and ways to develop them in the future:

_____
_____
_____

Yes No
☐   ☐

Are You Satisfied with Yourself Today:

Why : _____

_____

DATE: TIME :

OBSESSIVE COMPULSIVE PERSONALITY DISORDER
DAILY LOG

SITUATION / INTRUSIVE THOUGHTS :

MEANING OF THE INTRUSIVE THOUGHTS :

WHAT OCPD BEHAVIORS DID YOU DO ! !

Rate the Intensity of Obsessive Thoughts Today ○ ○ ○ ○ ○

MIND ENERGY : ☐ ☐ ☐

OCPD DBT WORKSHEET

TODAY'S FICKLE FEELINGS AND MY COPING SKILLS USED

CREATIVE OUTLETS TO REDUCE FEELINGS OF OBSESSION

THINGS TO WORK ON
(REALISTIC AND ACHIEVABLE THINGS)

THINGS I'M GRATEFUL FOR

IDEAS TO CONFRONT COMPULSIVE URGES

Date: / /

Sleep quality:

Daily Mood Checker

- [ ] ANGRY
- [ ] ANNOYED
- [ ] ANXIOUS
- [ ] ASHAMED
- [ ] AWKWARD
- [ ] BRAVE
- [ ] CALM
- [ ] CHEERFUL
- [ ] CHILL
- [ ] CONFUSED
- [ ] DISCOURAGED
- [ ] DISTRACTED
- [ ] EMBARRASSED
- [ ] EXCITED
- [ ] FRIENDLY
- [ ] GUILTY
- [ ] HAPPY
- [ ] HOPEFUL
- [ ] LONELY
- [ ] LOVED
- [ ] NERVOUS
- [ ] OFFENDED
- [ ] SCARED
- [ ] THOUGHTFUL
- [ ] TIRED
- [ ] UNCOMFORTABLE
- [ ] UNSURE

CHALLENGING OCPD SYMPTOMS DAILY ADVANCED WORKSHEET

CHALLENGE

_____

The self-destructive obsessive habits that I (felt , do) today ,Determine your level of success in dealing with it :

_____

_____

_____

_____

Social activities I have been involved in.
How much did this contribute to my psychological comfort:

_____

_____

_____

Write down the good things you discovered about your personality today after practicing your social life,Things related to your self-esteem, dignity, and ways to develop them in the future:

_____

_____

_____

Are You Satisfied with Yourself Today: Yes ☐ No ☐

Why : _____

_____

NEGATIVE BEHAVIORS THAT I SHOULD GET RID

MY PRIORITIES, MY BOUNDARIES RELATED TO MY RELATIONSHIPS WITH OTHERS

DAILY WINS AGAINST OCPD

WAYS TO MAKE TOMORROW BETTER

OCPD BEHAVIORS TO FIX OR IMPROVE

ATTENTION AND SHYNESS MANAGEMENT

DISTRESS TOLERANCE SKILLS:

COMMUNICATION SKILLS WITH OTHERS:

INTERPERSONAL CONFLICTS

OTHER THINGS

UPDATED ACADEMIC FACTS, INFORMATIONS, ABOUT THE OBSESSIVE COMPULSIVE PERSONALITY DISORDER

TV SHOWS, ACADEMIC ARTICLES, SCIENTIFIC BOOKS,...ETC

DATE: TIME :

OBSESSIVE COMPULSIVE PERSONALITY DISORDER
DAILY LOG

SITUATION / INTRUSIVE THOUGHTS :

_____

_____

MEANING OF THE INTRUSIVE THOUGHTS :

_____

_____

WHAT OCPD BEHAVIORS DID YOU DO ! !

_____

_____

_____

_____

Rate the Intensity of Obsessive Thoughts Today ○ ○ ○ ○ ○

MIND ENERGY : ☐ 🔋   ☐ 🔋   ☐ 🔋

OCPD DBT WORKSHEET

Date: / /

Sleep quality:

TODAY'S FICKLE FEELINGS AND MY COPING SKILLS USED

CREATIVE OUTLETS TO REDUCE FEELINGS OF OBSESSION

THINGS TO WORK ON
(REALISTIC AND ACHIEVABLE THINGS)

THINGS I'M GRATFUL FOR

IDEAS TO CONFRONT COMPULSIVE URGES

Daily Mood Checker

- [ ] ANGRY
- [ ] ANNOYED
- [ ] ANXIOUS
- [ ] ASHAMED
- [ ] AWKWARD
- [ ] BRAVE
- [ ] CALM
- [ ] CHEERFUL
- [ ] CHILL
- [ ] CONFUSED
- [ ] DISCOURAGED
- [ ] DISTRACTED
- [ ] EMBARRASSED
- [ ] EXCITED
- [ ] FRIENDLY
- [ ] GUILTY
- [ ] HAPPY
- [ ] HOPEFUL
- [ ] LONELY
- [ ] LOVED
- [ ] NERVOUS
- [ ] OFFENDED
- [ ] SCARED
- [ ] THOUGHTFUL
- [ ] TIRED
- [ ] UNCOMFORTABLE
- [ ] UNSURE

CHALLENGING OCPD SYMPTOMS DAILY ADVANCED WORKSHEET

CHALLENGE

The self-destructive obsessive habits that I (felt , do) today ,Determine your level of success in dealing with it :

_____

_____

_____

_____

Social activities I have been involved in.
How much did this contribute to my psychological comfort:

_____

_____

_____

Write down the good things you discovered about your personality today after practicing your social life,Things related to your self-esteem, dignity, and ways to develop them in the future:

_____

_____

_____

Are You Satisfied with Yourself Today: Yes ☐   No ☐

Why : _____

_____

DATE: TIME :

OBSESSIVE COMPULSIVE PERSONALITY DISORDER
DAILY LOG

SITUATION / INTRUSIVE THOUGHTS :

_____

_____

_____

MEANING OF THE INTRUSIVE THOUGHTS :

_____

_____

_____

WHAT OCPD BEHAVIORS DID YOU DO ! !

_____

_____

_____

_____

Rate the Intensity of Obsessive Thoughts Today   ○ ○ ○ ○ ○

| MIND ENERGY : | ☐ 🔋 | ☐ 🔋 | ☐ 🔋 |

OCPD DBT WORKSHEET

TODAY'S FICKLE FEELINGS AND MY COPING SKILLS USED

Date: / /
Sleep quality:

Daily Mood Checker

- ANGRY ☐
- ANNOYED ☐
- ANXIOUS ☐
- ASHAMED ☐
- AWKWARD ☐
- BRAVE ☐
- CALM ☐
- CHEERFUL ☐
- CHILL ☐
- CONFUSED ☐
- DISCOURAGED ☐
- DISTRACTED ☐
- EMBARRASSED ☐
- EXCITED ☐
- FRIENDLY ☐
- GUILTY ☐
- HAPPY ☐
- HOPEFUL ☐
- LONELY ☐
- LOVED ☐
- NERVOUS ☐
- OFFENDED ☐
- SCARED ☐
- THOUGHTFUL ☐
- TIRED ☐
- UNCOMFORTABLE ☐
- UNSURE ☐

CREATIVE OUTLETS TO REDUCE FEELINGS OF OBSESSION

**THINGS TO WORK ON
(REALISTIC AND ACHIEVABLE THINGS)**

THINGS I'M GRATEFUL FOR

IDEAS TO CONFRONT COMPULSIVE URGES

CHALLENGING OCPD SYMPTOMS DAILY ADVANCED WORKSHEET

CHALLENGE

The self-destructive obsessive habits that I (felt , do) today ,Determine your level of success in dealing with it :

_____
_____
_____
_____

Social activities I have been involved in.
How much did this contribute to my psychological comfort:

_____
_____
_____

Write down the good things you discovered about your personality today after practicing your social life,Things related to your self-esteem, dignity, and ways to develop them in the future:

_____
_____
_____

Are You Satisfied with Yourself Today: Yes ☐ No ☐

Why : _____

_____

NEGATIVE BEHAVIORS THAT I SHOULD GET RID

MY PRIORITIES, MY BOUNDARIES RELATED TO MY RELATIONSHIPS WITH OTHERS

DAILY WINS AGAINST OCPD

WAYS TO MAKE TOMORROW BETTER

OCPD BEHAVIORS TO FIX OR IMPROVE

ATTENTION AND SHYNESS MANAGEMENT

DISTRESS TOLERANCE SKILLS:

COMMUNICATION SKILLS WITH OTHERS:

INTERPERSONAL CONFLICTS

OTHER THINGS

UPDATED ACADEMIC FACTS, INFORMATIONS, ABOUT THE OBSESSIVE COMPULSIVE PERSONALITY DISORDER

TV SHOWS, ACADEMIC ARTICLES, SCIENTIFIC BOOKS,...ETC

DATE: *TIME :*

OBSESSIVE COMPULSIVE PERSONALITY DISORDER
DAILY LOG

SITUATION / INTRUSIVE THOUGHTS :

_____

_____

MEANING OF THE INTRUSIVE THOUGHTS :

_____

_____

WHAT OCPD BEHAVIORS DID YOU DO ! !

_____

_____

_____

_____

Rate the Intensity of Obsessive Thoughts Today   ○ ○ ○ ○ ○ ○

| MIND ENERGY : | ☐ 🔋 | ☐ 🔋 | ☐ 🔋 |

OCPD DBT WORKSHEET

TODAY'S FICKLE FEELINGS AND MY COPING SKILLS USED

Date: / /
Sleep quality:

Daily Mood Checker ✓

- ANGRY ☐
- ANNOYED ☐
- ANXIOUS ☐
- ASHAMED ☐
- AWKWARD ☐
- BRAVE ☐
- CALM ☐
- CHEERFUL ☐
- CHILL ☐
- CONFUSED ☐
- DISCOURAGED ☐
- DISTRACTED ☐
- EMBARRASSED ☐
- EXCITED ☐
- FRIENDLY ☐
- GUILTY ☐
- HAPPY ☐
- HOPEFUL ☐
- LONELY ☐
- LOVED ☐
- NERVOUS ☐
- OFFENDED ☐
- SCARED ☐
- THOUGHTFUL ☐
- TIRED ☐
- UNCOMFORTABLE ☐
- UNSURE ☐

CREATIVE OUTLETS TO REDUCE FEELINGS OF OBSESSION

THINGS TO WORK ON
(REALISTIC AND ACHIEVABLE THINGS)

THINGS I'M GRATEFUL FOR

IDEAS TO CONFRONT COMPULSIVE URGES

CHALLENGING OCPD SYMPTOMS DAILY ADVANCED WORKSHEET

CHALLENGE

The self-destructive obsessive habits that I (felt , do) today ,Determine your level of success in dealing with it :

_____
_____
_____
_____

Social activities I have been involved in.
How much did this contribute to my psychological comfort:

_____
_____
_____

Write down the good things you discovered about your personality today after practicing your social life,Things related to your self-esteem, dignity, and ways to develop them in the future:

_____
_____
_____

Are You Satisfied with Yourself Today: Yes ☐   No ☐

Why : _____

_____

DATE: TIME :

OBSESSIVE COMPULSIVE PERSONALITY DISORDER
DAILY LOG

SITUATION / INTRUSIVE THOUGHTS :

_____

_____

MEANING OF THE INTRUSIVE THOUGHTS :

_____

_____

WHAT OCPD BEHAVIORS DID YOU DO ! !

_____

_____

_____

_____

Rate the Intensity of Obsessive Thoughts Today   ○ ○ ○ ○ ○

MIND ENERGY :   ☐ 🔋   ☐ 🔋   ☐ 🔋

OCPD DBT WORKSHEET

TODAY'S FICKLE FEELINGS AND MY COPING SKILLS USED

CREATIVE OUTLETS TO REDUCE FEELINGS OF OBSESSION

THINGS TO WORK ON
(REALISTIC AND ACHIEVABLE THINGS)

THINGS I'M GRATEFUL FOR

IDEAS TO CONFRONT COMPULSIVE URGES

Date: / /
Sleep quality:

Daily Mood Checker ✓

- ANGRY ☐
- ANNOYED ☐
- ANXIOUS ☐
- ASHAMED ☐
- AWKWARD ☐
- BRAVE ☐
- CALM ☐
- CHEERFUL ☐
- CHILL ☐
- CONFUSED ☐
- DISCOURAGED ☐
- DISTRACTED ☐
- EMBARRASSED ☐
- EXCITED ☐
- FRIENDLY ☐
- GUILTY ☐
- HAPPY ☐
- HOPEFUL ☐
- LONELY ☐
- LOVED ☐
- NERVOUS ☐
- OFFENDED ☐
- SCARED ☐
- THOUGHTFUL ☐
- TIRED ☐
- UNCOMFORTABLE ☐
- UNSURE ☐

CHALLENGING OCPD SYMPTOMS DAILY ADVANCED WORKSHEET

CHALLENGE

The self-destructive obsessive habits that I (felt , do) today ,Determine your level of success in dealing with it :

_____
_____
_____
_____

Social activities I have been involved in.
How much did this contribute to my psychological comfort:

_____
_____
_____

Write down the good things you discovered about your personality today after practicing your social life,Things related to your self-esteem, dignity, and ways to develop them in the future:

_____
_____
_____

Are You Satisfied with Yourself Today: Yes ☐   No ☐

Why : _____
_____

NEGATIVE BEHAVIORS THAT I SHOULD GET RID

MY PRIORITIES, MY BOUNDARIES RELATED TO MY RELATIONSHIPS WITH OTHERS

DAILY WINS AGAINST OCPD

WAYS TO MAKE TOMORROW BETTER

OCPD BEHAVIORS TO FIX OR IMPROVE

ATTENTION AND SHYNESS MANAGEMENT

DISTRESS TOLERANCE SKILLS:

COMMUNICATION SKILLS WITH OTHERS:

INTERPERSONAL CONFLICTS

OTHER THINGS

UPDATED ACADEMIC FACTS, INFORMATIONS, ABOUT THE OBSESSIVE COMPULSIVE PERSONALITY DISORDER

TV SHOWS, ACADEMIC ARTICLES, SCIENTIFIC BOOKS,...ETC

DATE: TIME :

OBSESSIVE COMPULSIVE PERSONALITY DISORDER
DAILY LOG

SITUATION / INTRUSIVE THOUGHTS :

_____

_____

_____

MEANING OF THE INTRUSIVE THOUGHTS :

_____

_____

_____

WHAT OCPD BEHAVIORS DID YOU DO ! !

_____

_____

_____

_____

Rate the Intensity of Obsessive Thoughts Today   ○ ○ ○ ○ ○

| MIND ENERGY :   ☐ 🔋   ☐ 🔋   ☐ 🔋 |

OCPD DBT WORKSHEET

TODAY'S FICKLE FEELINGS AND MY COPING SKILLS USED

CREATIVE OUTLETS TO REDUCE FEELINGS OF OBSESSION

THINGS TO WORK ON
(REALISTIC AND ACHIEVABLE THINGS)

THINGS I'M GRATEFUL FOR

IDEAS TO CONFRONT COMPULSIVE URGES

Date: / /

Sleep quality:

Daily Mood Checker ✓

- ☐ ANGRY
- ☐ ANNOYED
- ☐ ANXIOUS
- ☐ ASHAMED
- ☐ AWKWARD
- ☐ BRAVE
- ☐ CALM
- ☐ CHEERFUL
- ☐ CHILL
- ☐ CONFUSED
- ☐ DISCOURAGED
- ☐ DISTRACTED
- ☐ EMBARRASSED
- ☐ EXCITED
- ☐ FRIENDLY
- ☐ GUILTY
- ☐ HAPPY
- ☐ HOPEFUL
- ☐ LONELY
- ☐ LOVED
- ☐ NERVOUS
- ☐ OFFENDED
- ☐ SCARED
- ☐ THOUGHTFUL
- ☐ TIRED
- ☐ UNCOMFORTABLE
- ☐ UNSURE

CHALLENGING OCPD SYMPTOMS DAILY ADVANCED WORKSHEET

CHALLENGE

The self-destructive obsessive habits that I (felt , do) today ,Determine your level of success in dealing with it :

_____
_____
_____
_____

Social activities I have been involved in.
How much did this contribute to my psychological comfort:

_____
_____
_____

Write down the good things you discovered about your personality today after practicing your social life,Things related to your self-esteem, dignity, and ways to develop them in the future:

_____
_____
_____

Are You Satisfied with Yourself Today: Yes ☐ No ☐

Why : _____

_____

DATE: TIME :

OBSESSIVE COMPULSIVE PERSONALITY DISORDER
DAILY LOG

SITUATION / INTRUSIVE THOUGHTS :

_____

_____

MEANING OF THE INTRUSIVE THOUGHTS :

_____

_____

WHAT OCPD BEHAVIORS DID YOU DO ! !

_____

_____

_____

_____

Rate the Intensity of Obsessive Thoughts Today ○ ○ ○ ○ ○ ○

MIND ENERGY : ▫🔋 ▫🔋 ▫🔋

OCPD DBT WORKSHEET

TODAY'S FICKLE FEELINGS AND MY COPING SKILLS USED

Date: / /

Sleep quality:

Daily Mood Checker ✓

- ANGRY ☐
- ANNOYED ☐
- ANXIOUS ☐
- ASHAMED ☐
- AWKWARD ☐
- BRAVE ☐
- CALM ☐
- CHEERFUL ☐
- CHILL ☐
- CONFUSED ☐
- DISCOURAGED ☐
- DISTRACTED ☐
- EMBARRASSED ☐
- EXCITED ☐
- FRIENDLY ☐
- GUILTY ☐
- HAPPY ☐
- HOPEFUL ☐
- LONELY ☐
- LOVED ☐
- NERVOUS ☐
- OFFENDED ☐
- SCARED ☐
- THOUGHTFUL ☐
- TIRED ☐
- UNCOMFORTABLE ☐
- UNSURE ☐

CREATIVE OUTLETS TO REDUCE FEELINGS OF OBSESSION

THINGS TO WORK ON
(REALISTIC AND ACHIEVABLE THINGS)

THINGS I'M GRATEFUL FOR

IDEAS TO CONFRONT COMPULSIVE URGES

CHALLENGING OCPD SYMPTOMS DAILY ADVANCED WORKSHEET

CHALLENGE

The self-destructive obsessive habits that I (felt , do) today ,Determine your level of success in dealing with it :

_____
_____
_____
_____

Social activities I have been involved in.
How much did this contribute to my psychological comfort:

_____
_____
_____

Write down the good things you discovered about your personality today after practicing your social life,Things related to your self-esteem, dignity, and ways to develop them in the future:

_____
_____
_____

Are You Satisfied with Yourself Today: Yes ☐   No ☐

Why : _____

_____

NEGATIVE BEHAVIORS THAT I SHOULD GET RID

MY PRIORITIES, MY BOUNDARIES RELATED TO MY RELATIONSHIPS WITH OTHERS

DAILY WINS AGAINST OCPD

WAYS TO MAKE TOMORROW BETTER

OCPD BEHAVIORS TO FIX OR IMPROVE

ATTENTION AND SHYNESS MANAGEMENT

DISTRESS TOLERANCE SKILLS:

COMMUNICATION SKILLS WITH OTHERS:

INTERPERSONAL CONFLICTS

OTHER THINGS

UPDATED ACADEMIC FACTS, INFORMATIONS, ABOUT THE OBSESSIVE COMPULSIVE PERSONALITY DISORDER

TV SHOWS, ACADEMIC ARTICLES, SCIENTIFIC BOOKS,...ETC

DATE: TIME:

OBSESSIVE COMPULSIVE PERSONALITY DISORDER
DAILY LOG

SITUATION / INTRUSIVE THOUGHTS :

_____
_____
_____

MEANING OF THE INTRUSIVE THOUGHTS :

_____
_____
_____

WHAT OCPD BEHAVIORS DID YOU DO ! !

_____
_____
_____
_____

Rate the Intensity of Obsessive Thoughts Today ○ ○ ○ ○ ○ ○

| MIND ENERGY : | ☐ 🔋 | ☐ 🔋 | ☐ 🔋 |

OCPD DBT WORKSHEET

Date: / /

Sleep quality:

TODAY'S FICKLE FEELINGS AND MY COPING SKILLS USED

CREATIVE OUTLETS TO REDUCE FEELINGS OF OBSESSION

THINGS TO WORK ON
(REALISTIC AND ACHIEVABLE THINGS)

THINGS I'M GRATEFUL FOR

IDEAS TO CONFRONT COMPULSIVE URGES

Daily Mood Checker ✓

- ANGRY ☐
- ANNOYED ☐
- ANXIOUS ☐
- ASHAMED ☐
- AWKWARD ☐
- BRAVE ☐
- CALM ☐
- CHEERFUL ☐
- CHILL ☐
- CONFUSED ☐
- DISCOURAGED ☐
- DISTRACTED ☐
- EMBARRASSED ☐
- EXCITED ☐
- FRIENDLY ☐
- GUILTY ☐
- HAPPY ☐
- HOPEFUL ☐
- LONELY ☐
- LOVED ☐
- NERVOUS ☐
- OFFENDED ☐
- SCARED ☐
- THOUGHTFUL ☐
- TIRED ☐
- UNCOMFORTABLE ☐
- UNSURE ☐

CHALLENGING OCPD SYMPTOMS DAILY ADVANCED WORKSHEET

CHALLENGE

The self-destructive obsessive habits that I (felt , do) today ,Determine your level of success in dealing with it :

_____
_____
_____

Social activities I have been involved in.
How much did this contribute to my psychological comfort:

_____
_____
_____

Write down the good things you discovered about your personality today after practicing your social life,Things related to your self-esteem, dignity, and ways to develop them in the future:

_____
_____
_____

Are You Satisfied with Yourself Today: Yes ☐ No ☐

Why : _____

_____

DATE: TIME :

OBSESSIVE COMPULSIVE PERSONALITY DISORDER
DAILY LOG

SITUATION / INTRUSIVE THOUGHTS :

_____

_____

_____

MEANING OF THE INTRUSIVE THOUGHTS :

_____

_____

_____

WHAT OCPD BEHAVIORS DID YOU DO ! !

_____

_____

_____

_____

Rate the Intensity of Obsessive Thoughts Today   ○ ○ ○ ○ ○

MIND ENERGY :   ☐ 🔋   ☐ 🔋   ☐ 🔋

OCPD DBT WORKSHEET

TODAY'S FICKLE FEELINGS AND MY COPING SKILLS USED

Date: / /
Sleep quality:

Daily Mood Checker ✓

- ANGRY ☐
- ANNOYED ☐
- ANXIOUS ☐
- ASHAMED ☐
- AWKWARD ☐
- BRAVE ☐
- CALM ☐
- CHEERFUL ☐
- CHILL ☐
- CONFUSED ☐
- DISCOURAGED ☐
- DISTRACTED ☐
- EMBARRASSED ☐
- EXCITED ☐
- FRIENDLY ☐
- GUILTY ☐
- HAPPY ☐
- HOPEFUL ☐
- LONELY ☐
- LOVED ☐
- NERVOUS ☐
- OFFENDED ☐
- SCARED ☐
- THOUGHTFUL ☐
- TIRED ☐
- UNCOMFORTABLE ☐
- UNSURE ☐

CREATIVE OUTLETS TO REDUCE FEELINGS OF OBSESSION

THINGS TO WORK ON
(REALISTIC AND ACHIEVABLE THINGS)

THINGS I'M GRATEFUL FOR

IDEAS TO CONFRONT COMPULSIVE URGES

CHALLENGING OCPD SYMPTOMS DAILY ADVANCED WORKSHEET

CHALLENGE

The self-destructive obsessive habits that I (felt , do) today ,Determine your level of success in dealing with it :

_____
_____
_____
_____

Social activities I have been involved in.
How much did this contribute to my psychological comfort:

_____
_____
_____

Write down the good things you discovered about your personality today after practicing your social life,Things related to your self-esteem, dignity, and ways to develop them in the future:

_____
_____
_____

Are You Satisfied with Yourself Today: Yes ☐ No ☐

Why : _____

_____

DATE: TIME:

OBSESSIVE COMPULSIVE PERSONALITY DISORDER
DAILY LOG

SITUATION / INTRUSIVE THOUGHTS :

_____

_____

MEANING OF THE INTRUSIVE THOUGHTS :

_____

_____

WHAT OCPD BEHAVIORS DID YOU DO ! !

_____

_____

_____

_____

Rate the Intensity of Obsessive Thoughts Today ○ ○ ○ ○ ○

| MIND ENERGY : | ☐ 🔋 | ☐ 🔋 | ☐ 🔋 |

OCPD DBT WORKSHEET

TODAY'S FICKLE FEELINGS AND MY COPING SKILLS USED

Date: / /

Sleep quality:

Daily Mood Checker

- [ ] ANGRY
- [ ] ANNOYED
- [ ] ANXIOUS
- [ ] ASHAMED
- [ ] AWKWARD
- [ ] BRAVE
- [ ] CALM
- [ ] CHEERFUL
- [ ] CHILL
- [ ] CONFUSED
- [ ] DISCOURAGED
- [ ] DISTRACTED
- [ ] EMBARRASSED
- [ ] EXCITED
- [ ] FRIENDLY
- [ ] GUILTY
- [ ] HAPPY
- [ ] HOPEFUL
- [ ] LONELY
- [ ] LOVED
- [ ] NERVOUS
- [ ] OFFENDED
- [ ] SCARED
- [ ] THOUGHTFUL
- [ ] TIRED
- [ ] UNCOMFORTABLE
- [ ] UNSURE

CREATIVE OUTLETS TO REDUCE FEELINGS OF OBSESSION

THINGS TO WORK ON
(REALISTIC AND ACHIEVABLE THINGS)

THINGS I'M GRATEFUL FOR

IDEAS TO CONFRONT COMPULSIVE URGES

CHALLENGING OCPD SYMPTOMS DAILY ADVANCED WORKSHEET

CHALLENGE

The self-destructive obsessive habits that I (felt , do) today ,Determine your level of success in dealing with it :

_____

_____

_____

_____

Social activities I have been involved in.
How much did this contribute to my psychological comfort:

_____

_____

_____

Write down the good things you discovered about your personality today after practicing your social life,Things related to your self-esteem, dignity, and ways to develop them in the future:

_____

_____

_____

Are You Satisfied with Yourself Today: Yes ☐ No ☐

Why : _____

_____

DATE: TIME :

OBSESSIVE COMPULSIVE PERSONALITY DISORDER
DAILY LOG

SITUATION / INTRUSIVE THOUGHTS :

MEANING OF THE INTRUSIVE THOUGHTS :

WHAT OCPD BEHAVIORS DID YOU DO ! !

Rate the Intensity of Obsessive Thoughts Today ○ ○ ○ ○ ○

MIND ENERGY :

OCPD DBT WORKSHEET

TODAY'S FICKLE FEELINGS AND MY COPING SKILLS USED

Date: / /

Sleep quality:

Daily Mood Checker ✓

- ANGRY ☐
- ANNOYED ☐
- ANXIOUS ☐
- ASHAMED ☐
- AWKWARD ☐
- BRAVE ☐
- CALM ☐
- CHEERFUL ☐
- CHILL ☐
- CONFUSED ☐
- DISCOURAGED ☐
- DISTRACTED ☐
- EMBARRASSED ☐
- EXCITED ☐
- FRIENDLY ☐
- GUILTY ☐
- HAPPY ☐
- HOPEFUL ☐
- LONELY ☐
- LOVED ☐
- NERVOUS ☐
- OFFENDED ☐
- SCARED ☐
- THOUGHTFUL ☐
- TIRED ☐
- UNCOMFORTABLE ☐
- UNSURE ☐

CREATIVE OUTLETS TO REDUCE FEELINGS OF OBSESSION

THINGS TO WORK ON
(REALISTIC AND ACHIEVABLE THINGS)

THINGS I'M GRATFUL FOR

IDEAS TO CONFRONT COMPULSIVE URGES

CHALLENGING OCPD SYMPTOMS DAILY ADVANCED WORKSHEET

CHALLENGE

The self-destructive obsessive habits that I (felt , do) today ,Determine your level of success in dealing with it :

_____
_____
_____
_____

Social activities I have been involved in.
How much did this contribute to my psychological comfort:

_____
_____
_____

Write down the good things you discovered about your personality today after practicing your social life,Things related to your self-esteem, dignity, and ways to develop them in the future:

_____
_____
_____

Are You Satisfied with Yourself Today: Yes ☐ No ☐

Why : _____
_____

Made in United States
North Haven, CT
02 June 2023

37293512R00098